A SHORT INT  TEX

BY

FIRUZA KARMALI (AIBARA)

◇
A
BOOK FOR
THOSE WHO
ARE COMPLETELY
NEW TO LaTeX AND
WANT TO EXPLORE.
HAPPY READ-
ING TO ALL
MY READ-
ERS.
◇

2018

ii

Preface

I welcome all my readers of this book, 'A Short Introduction to LaTeX'. The purpose of writing this book is to make people (especially writers) aware of LaTeX, a document preparation system which was initially developed by Leslie Lamport.

Usually, writers prefer to write their content in plain text files rather than using WYSIWYG (What You See Is What You Get) editors, so as to concentrate on the text and not the way it looks. LaTeX provides the same facility which the writers need uniform formatting is achieved by using some basic commands.

Moreover, LaTeXis free, can be used on most of the operating systems (like Unix, Linux, Windows, Mac, etc.) and is licensed under the LaTeX Project Public License.

This book is specifically written for novice learners who want to explore this subject and start writing content using LaTeX. I wish all my readers the very best!

Firuza Karmali
aka
Firuza Aibara

iv

Acknowledgements

I would like to thank my family (Mom, Dad, and Husband) who has always been very supportive in any task that I do and have always encouraged me to listen to my heart.

I especially thank my Mom who so willingly proof-read my book in spite of her busy schedule. This book was impossible without her comments and suggestions to improve the language and tone of the text.

I would like to thank Amazon for facilitating a platform (Kindly Direct Publishing) where authors like me are empowered to publish books and reach out to the public.

Last but not least, I thank all my readers for always keeping me motivated and for reading my books. Thank you for your extended support as always.

Dedication

I dedicate this book to Prof. Uday Gaitonde who has been using LaTeX and TeX much before I was born. He always loved to discuss new ideas, engaged me in solving problems, and each time encouraged me to learn something new about LaTeX.

I also dedicate this book to Prof. Kannan Moudgalya who has been a source of inspiration for people (including me) who wanted to learn LaTeX and to use it effectively in our assignments and daily writing activities.

Last but not the least I dedicate this book to Nagesh Karmali (my loving husband) who forced me to learn LaTeX and made me believe that it is more useful and promising for writing documents, reports, books, posters, etc..

Contents

List of Tables

List of Figures

Chapter 1
Document
Structure

What you will learn

1.1 Introduction

LaTeX is a document preparation system for typesetting program. It is used to create different types of document structures. A LaTeX file (.tex) is created using any text editor (vim, emacs, gedit, etc.). There are also many LaTeX IDEs like Kile, TexStudio, etc..[2]

The code is then compiled which creates a standard (.pdf) file. Thus, the presentation of a document does not change on different machines.

| .tex File (Input) | pdflatex .tex (Compile) | .pdf File (Output) |

Figure 1.1: Creation process

This book introduces LaTeX and gives an overview of what can be achieved. It can be used as a quick reference guide. Refer to the wiki book or to the references given at the end of this book for a detailed explanation and to explore different styles.

LaTeX allows users to concentrate on the content, rather than the presentation of content. It does not follow the standard approach of What You See Is What You Get (WYSIWYG). Predefined styles are embedded into different packages, which allows the users/authors to use the styles, by including that package into the (.tex) file.

The following sections of this chapter include the usage of various document classes, packages, how to structure a document, section numbering, and designing the table of contents. [3]

1.2   Setup

1.2.1   Installation

Ubuntu/Debian Install using the following command
`sudo apt-get install texlive-full`.

Windows Install miktex from `https://miktex.org/download` and follow the steps.

Thereafter, proceed to install the desired LaTeX IDE.

1.2.2 Build and View

Manually: Assume that one is using a simple text editor like 'notepad' or 'gedit'. Save the file with '.tex' extention. Build the file using `pdflatex filename.tex`. This will generate .pdf file.

LATEX IDE: Most LATEX IDEs have side by side editor and a pdf viewer. Click 'Build' or 'Build and View' button to build .tex files.

1.3 Overview of LATEX File

A LATEX file consists of the following:

1. Document Class and Package: Here one mentions what type of a document it is and the packages needed

2. Document Information: Here one mentions the initial information of the document, i.e. title, author, date, etc.

3. Document: This is nothing but the actual content.

All of these are explained below in detail.

1.3.1 Document Class and Packages

LATEX provides different document classes (Article, Book, Report, IEEETran) for writing different types of documents. Along with the type of document, the size of paper and font size may also be specified. This is mentioned below.

```
\documentclass[a4paper,11pt]
    {article|book|report|ieeetran}
```

The size of paper can be a2paper, a3paper, a4paper, a5paper, etc..

1.3.2   Document Information

The first page of a document usually comprises of title, author, date, etc.. These details are mentioned after creating the document class.

```
% Note that % is comment.
% The text following the % is not compiled
\title{Title of your Document}
\author{Name1 \\ Name2}
%( \\ represents new line)
\date{\today}
```

1.3.3   Document Structure

The skeleton of a typical document structure is given below:

```
\begin{document}
    \maketitle
    \chapter{Chapter Title}
    \section{Title}
    \subsection{Title}
    \subsubsection{Title}
    \paragraph{Title}
\end{document}
```

1.4   Putting it all together

1.4.1   Creating .tex file

```
\documentclass[10pt]{article}
\title{A Short Introduction to LaTeX}
\author{Firuza Aibara}
\begin{document}
    \maketitle
    \section{Document Structure}
    \subsection{Introduction}
    \paragraph{}
```

```
    A document preparation system for ...
    \subsection{Setup}
    \subsubsection{Installation}
    \paragraph{}
    To install \LaTeX ...
  \end{document}
```

1.4.2   Building and Viewing

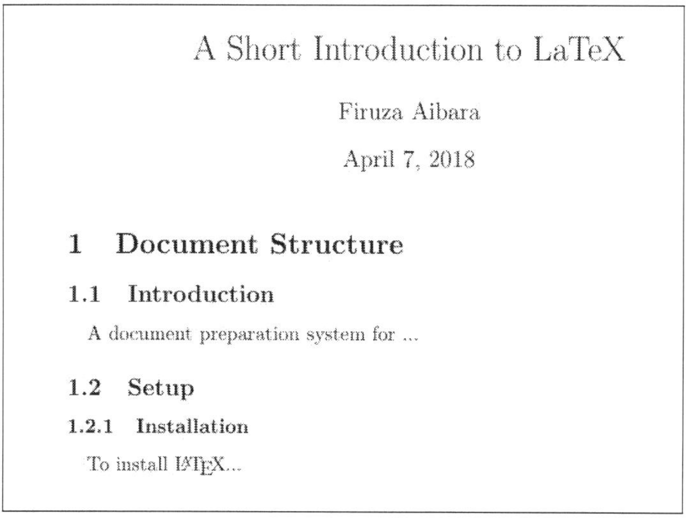

A Short Introduction to LaTeX

Firuza Aibara

April 7, 2018

1   Document Structure

1.1   Introduction

A document preparation system for ...

1.2   Setup

1.2.1   Installation

To install LaTeX...

Figure 1.2: PDF file

1.5   Sections

1.5.1   Section Levels

A document is divided into different (Level Name/Sections) like chapters, sections, subsections, etc.. Every section is associated with a level number. Not all sections are included in all document classes. The table given below mentions the different sections with their corresponding level numbers and the document classes in which they can be used.

Level	LevelName / Sections	Article	Report	Book	IEEEtran
-	\begin{abstract}...\end{abstract}	✔	✔	✗	✔
-1	\part{Title}	✔	✔	✔	✗
0	\chapter{Title}	✗	✔	✔	✗
1	\section{Title}	✔	✔	✔	✔
2	\subsection{Title}	✔	✔	✔	✔
3	\subsubsection{Title}	✔	✔	✔	✔
4	\paragraph{Title}	✔	✔	✔	✔
5	\subparagraph{Title}	✔	✔	✔	✔

Table 1.1: Document class and its sections

1.5.2   Numbering the Sections

In a document, only Level -1 to Level 3 are numbered by default. 'Paragraph' and 'Subparagraph' are not numbered. In order to change this, before the \begin{document}, the setcounter command is used as shown below.

```
\setcounter{secnumdepth}{<LevelNo.>}
```

E.g. The following command, numbers the paragraphs in the document.

```
\setcounter{secnumdepth}{4}
```

1.6   ToC (Table of Contents)

ToC is generated by using \tableofcontents command.

1.6.1   Depth of ToC

By default, the ToC that is generated, is till level 3 i.e. till 'Subsections'. Inorder to change this, before the \begin{document}, the `setcounter` command is used as shown below.

```
\setcounter{tocdepth}{<LevelNo.>}
```

E.g. The following command changes the depth of ToC to subparagraphs.

```
\setcounter{tocdepth}{5}
```

1.6.2   Unnumbered Section and Hide in ToC

There are certain situations when one does not want to number the sections nor display the section name in ToC. To achieve this, '*' is mentioned after the `section` command. By using the following command, the subsection titled, 'Features of the System' will be unnumbered and will not be displayed in the table of contents.

```
\subsection*{Features of the System}
```

1.6.3   Display Unnumbered Section in ToC

`addcontentsline` command is used to display an unnumbered section/level in ToC. This is shown below:

```
\addcontentsline{toc}{<Section>}
  {Name that you want to display}
```

E.g.

```
\subsection*{Pen}
\addcontentsline{toc}{subsection}{Pen}
```

1.6.4   Display an Alias of any Section in ToC

To display an alternative name for any section/level, write the alias in box bracket after the command. An example is given below.

```
\subsection[Display Short Topic Name]
    {Very Large Topic Name which is
        too big to be displayed in ToC}
```

1.7   Exercises

1. Recall the different document classes discussed. Are these the only classes available? If not, then find out.

2. Consider that you had been on a field trip and you have been asked to summarize the events. You are thinking of creating parts for each day. Which document class will you prefer to use?

3. The title of one of the subsections is too long, which does not look good in Table of contents. What should I do?

4. Consider the following LaTeXcode. The section number of 'Introduction' is displayed as 0.1, instead of 1. What could be the possible error?

```
\documentclass{book}
\begin{document}
    \section{Introduction}
\end{document}
```

What you can do

1. Install LaTeX and IDEs.

2. Create a simple LaTeX document.

3. Build and view it.

4. Use different document classes.

5. Define different paper sizes.

6. Generate Table of Contents.

7. Divide/Organize document into chapters, section, subsections, etc.

Chapter 2
Formatting Pages

What you will learn

This chapter includes the different parameters that are required to format the page, such as setting margins, single or double sided document, page numbers (including even and odd), orientation of page, multi-column document, etc.. [4] Most of the formatting given in this chapter requires the use of 'Geometry' package. It is mentioned at appropriate places.

13

2.1   Size

The size of the paper needs to be mentioned while creating the documentclass. The different sizes are a0paper to a6paper, b0paper to b6paper, legalpaper, executivepaper, etc.. Along with the size, there is also an option to specify whether your document is a single-sided document or a two-sided document. The difference between them is, that two-sided documents have different styles for even and odd pages; whereas, for a single-sided document, all pages have the same style. By default, most of the document classes are single-sided, while 'books' are two-sided. The following example creates a two-sided article of a3 paper size.

```
\documentclass[a3paper,twoside]{article}
```

2.2   Margins

Margins are specified using a package called 'Geometry'. There are many methods for setting margins, of which 2 are given below:

```
Example 1: All margins are of 1 inch
\usepackage[margin=1in]{geometry}

Example 2: Each margin of different size
\usepackage[top=1in, bottom=0.75in,
   left=1.25in, right=1.1in]{geometry}
```

For a two-sided document, even and odd page margins can be set using inner and outer, instead of left and right. Consider an example given below.

```
\documentclass[a4paper,twoside]{article}
     OR
\documentclass[a4paper]{book}
\usepackage[inner=2in,outer=1in,top=1in,
   bottom=1in]{geometry}
```

The margin for top and bottom is 1 inch for all the pages.

The margins for odd and even pages are shown in the table given below. Usually, for all odd pages left margin is greater than right; while for even pages, the right margin is bigger than left.

Margin Pages	Left (in)	Right (in)
Odd	2	1
Even	1	2

Table 2.1: Margins for odd and even pages

2.3   Page Style and Numbering

2.3.1   Basic Page Style

Styling of a page defines the way headers and footers are displayed and the information they contain. Page style can be set for the entire document or only for the current page.

For entire document: `\pagestyle{<style>}`
For current page: `\thispagestyle{<style>}`

Style	Header	Footer
empty	✗	✗
plain	✗	Page number
headings	Section name and page number	✗
myheadings	Page number. Other text if needed can also be added.	✗

Table 2.2: Page Styles

2.3.2   Page Style using Fancy

The `fancy` package is used to customize the headers and footers.

```
\usepackage{fancyhdr}
\pagestyle{fancy}
```

The commands given in the table 2.3 are used to set header and footer based on the desired alignment.

Alignment	Header	Footer
Left	\lhead{...}	\lfoot{...}
Center	\chead{...}	\cfoot{...}
Right	\rhead{...}	\rfoot{...}

Table 2.3: Header and footer using `fancy` package

Given below is a list of commands that are used to insert information about the document. These can be used independently in a document or can be embedded in header or footer.

Command	Denotes the Current
\thepage	Page number
\chaptername	title 'Chapter'
\thechapter	Chapter number
\thesection	Section number
\usepackage{lastpage} \pageref{LastPage}	Total number of pages

Table 2.4: Information about the document

E.g.

```
\rhead{\thesection}
\rfoot{\thepage of \pageref{LastPage}}
```

2.3.3 Numbering Style

\pagenumbering command is used to specify the styles of page numbers.

```
\pagenumbering{arabic|roman|Roman|alph|
    Alph}
```

Whenever this command is encountered, the page numbering (irrespective of the style given above), will always start from 1. i.e. for 'roman' style, the numbering will start from 'i'.

2.3.4 Reset Page Number

The page numbers are reset using the \setcounter command. The page numbering will continue from this page number, for the rest of the pages.

```
\setcounter{page}{<Number>}
\setcounter{page}{4}
```

2.4 Orientation

Orientation of a page is either portrait (by default) or landscape. The orientation of entire document or a specific part in the document can be changed to landscape. Given below are 2 such examples.

2.4.1 Landscape (Entire Document)

The orientation of an entire document can be changed to landscape using any of the 2 options given below:

```
1. \documentclass[landscape,a4...]{...} OR
2. \usepackage[landscape]{geometry}
```

2.4.2   Landscape (Specific Part)

```
\usepackage{lscape | pdflscape}
\begin{landscape}
    ...   % The content that you want
    ...   % to be displayed as landscape
\end{landscape}
```

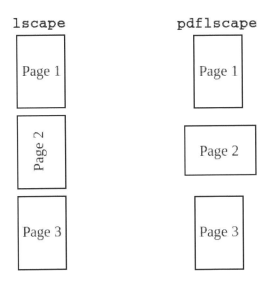

Figure 2.1: lscape Vs pdflscape

This will create content in landscape form. The difference between lscape and pdflscape is that, lscape rotates the content by 90 degrees, but not the page; while the package pdflatex rotates the entire page. Rest of the pages remain portrait.

2.5   Page Breaks

\pagebreak or \newpage commands are used to begin the content on a new page. The difference between them is that pagebreak stretches out the paragraphs to cover the entire page, while newpage just ends the current page and takes a new one. The following shows the difference graphically.

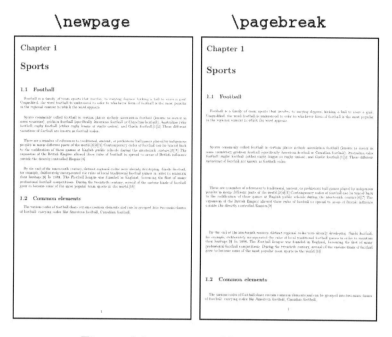

Figure 2.2: newpage Vs pagebreak

2.6 Columns

Usually, a document has content which is organized in a single column, unlike research papers which have 2 columns or a large page which needs to be divided into multiple columns, like a newspaper.

2.6.1 Two Columns

The `twocolumn` attribute is used to divide the entire document into two columns.

```
\documentclass[a4paper,twocolumn]{article}
```

2.6.2 Multiple Columns – multicol package

`multicol` package is used to divide specific content into multiple columns.

```
\usepackage{multicol}
\begin{multicols}{<No. of Columns>}
        ...
\end{multicols}
```

Column Spacing

\columnsep command is used to increase/decrease the spacing by X points between the columns. The syntax is as follows.

```
\setlength\columnsep{<X>pt}
\begin{multicols}{<No. of Columns>} ...
```

Column Separator

\columnseprule command is used to divide a column with a vertical line. The syntax is as follows.

```
\setlength{\columnseprule}{<X>pt}
\begin{multicols}{<No. of Columns>} ...
```

Column Break

\columnbreak command is used to forcefully place the text mentioned after into the next column.

The limitation of this package is, that one cannot specify the size of the columns; all columns have equal width.

2.6.3 Multiple Columns – parcolumns package

parcolumns package, similar to multicols divides specific content into multiple columns. The sloppy command is used to adjust spacing. By default it is set to false i.e. it is not considered.

```
\usepackage{parcolumns}
\begin{parcolumns}{<No. of columns>}
  \colchunk{% column 1
    \sloppy ...   }
```

```
   . . .
   \colchunk{% column N
     \sloppy ...
   }
\end{parcolumns}
```

Column Separator

rulebetween option is specified as True if a column separator is needed. By default it is set to false. The syntax is as follows.

```
\begin{parcolumns}[rulebetween=true]
                   {<No. of columns>}
   . . .
\end{parcolumns}
```

Column Size

colwidths option is used to specify the size of the column. Starting with column 1, the sizes are specified in curly braces. By default, all columns have equal width. The syntax is as follows.

```
\begin{parcolumns}[colwidths=
                   {1=Xcm,2=Ycm}]{2}
. . .
\end{parcolumns}
```

Rather than specifying the size in cm, a better way would be to specify size with respect to text width. An example is given below:

```
\begin{parcolumns}[colwidths=
   {1=.4\textwidth,2=.2\textwidth,
   3=.3\textwidth}]{3}
. . .
\end{parcolumns}
```

Column Spacing

`distance` option is used to increase/decrease the spacing by X em between the columns. By default it is 2em. The syntax is as follows. This option does not go very well with `colwidths` option.

```
\begin{parcolumns}[distance=Xpt]
                 {<No. of columns>}
. . .
\end{parcolumns}
```

2.7   Footnotes

Footnotes provide some extra information about the content to the reader. It is usually placed at the bottom of the page (just above the footer). They are defined as follows:

```
Some text \footnote{Text that you want to
    display in the footline}
```

More information on customizing footnotes is given in [5].

2.8   Widows and Orphans

A continuation of the previous paragraph/content (usually a word or a single line) that appears on the next page is known as a widow; while the beginning of a sentence or paragraph that appears at the bottom of the page, with its continuation on the next page is termed as an orphan. [6]. Whether a widow or an orphan, it separates the content (line) from the main content (paragraph). Hence, a document should not contain widows or orphans. LaTeX usually takes care of it, but sometimes one may need to consider this by either manually putting page breaks or using the following command:

```
\widowpenalty=X
\clubpenalty=X
```

By default, X is 150, which can be increased to maximum 10000.

2.9 Exercises

1. Create a book having the following:

   - A title page without number
   - ToC having small roman page numbers
   - Chapters and sections with arabic page numbers

2. Create an article having the following:

   - any custom margins
   - Right header: section number and name
   - Left footer: page number and total pages

3. Create a book having page numbers as `ChapterNo-PageNo`. Every chapter should begin with page number 1.

4. You are required to create a pamphlet of A5 size (something similar to what is given below), which is to be distributed to the members of a certain group.

---

1 Introduction

The great variety of delicate and beautiful flowers has inspired the works of numerous poets, especially from the 18th-19th century Romantic era.

Famous examples include William Wordsworth's I Wandered Lonely as a Cloud and William Blake's Ah! Sun-Flower. Because of their varied and colorful appearance, flowers have long been a favorite subject of visual artists as well.

2 More Details

Flowers provide less food than other major plants parts (seeds, fruits, roots, stems and leaves) but they provide several important foods and spices. Flower vegetables include broccoli, cauliflower and artichoke. The most expensive spice is saffron [1]. Other flower spices are cloves and capers. Hops flowers are used to flavor beer. Marigold flowers are fed to chickens to give their egg yolks a golden yellow color, which consumers find more desirable; dried and ground marigold flowers are also used as a spice and colouring agent in Georgian-cuisine.

3 Food for Thought

Flowers of the dandelion and elder are often made into wine. Bee pollen, pollen collected from bees, is considered a health food by some people.

What you can do

1. Specify the size of the paper.

2. Set margins using the geometry package.

3. Add header and footer using different styles.

4. Customize header and footer using the fancy package.

5. Specify the style of the page number (arabic, roman, etc.).

6. Specify landscape orientation of an entire document or only a part.

7. Divide entire or only a part of a document into 2 or more columns using multicols and parcolumns package. Customize different parameters like column separator, etc.

8. Specify footnotes if needed.

9. Avoiding widows and orphans.

Chapter 3
Formatting Text

What you will learn

1. Correct way to use punctuation marks

2. Various text attributes like size, color, and alignment

3. Handle spaces between sections, text, etc.

4. Add bullets, numbers, or custom icons to points

5. Format code, mathematical expressions

This chapter covers the different ways of formatting text, like font size, font face, colors, aligning and spacing the content, making points, write codes and mathematics, etc., in the document. For detailed information please refer to the links given in [7] [8] [9].

3.1 Punctuation Marks

Quotation Marks: Generally for quoting texts we use '...' or "...". Latex considers ' and " as ending of the quotes. The correct way of writing is `` `...' `` and `` ``...'' ``.

Hyphen: Usually used to join or separate two words.
E.g. computer-aided design

En Dash: Usually used while mentioning range (range of pages, years, etc.) or relationships, etc.. `\textendash` command is used to create a endash. E.g. Served from: 1991`\textendash` 2002 (Served from: 1991–2002)

Em Dash: It is usually used in place of a colon, parentheses, etc.. `\textemdash` command is used to create an em dash in latex. E.g. "Description begins in the writer's imagination, but should finish in the reader's. `\textemdash` Stephen King" (... —Stephen King)

Ellipsis: A series of 3 dots that are displayed, usually to denote some text which is not written. E.g. 10, 20, ..., 90, 100. In latex, this can be written as 10, 20, `\ldots`, 90, 100.

3.2 Text Attribute and Font Size

The font size for article, report, and book document classes is 10pt, 11pt, or 12pt. This is mentioned as given below:

```
\documentclass[Xpt]{article|report|book}
```

With respect to the font size defined in the document class, the font size can be increased/decreased using LaTeX commands. For example `\Huge`, `\large`, etc.. The default font size is `\normalsize`. This command is used to revert back to the default size. To change the font size of just a few lines, then the text must be enclosed in curly braces. E.g. { `\Huge` ... }. In this case, there is no need to revert back to the default one. The absolute font size is given below:

Font Styles		Font size			
Style	**Command**	**Size**	**10pt**	**11pt**	**12pt**
Bold	\textbf{...}	tiny	5	6	6
Italics	\textit{...}	scriptsize	7	8	8
Emphasis	\emph{...}	footnotesize	8	9	10
<u>Underline</u>	\underline{...}	small	9	10	10.95
Sᴍᴀʟʟ Cᴀᴘs	\textsc{...}	normalsize	10	10.95	12
Roman	\textrm{...}	large	12	12	14.4
Sans Serif	\textsf{...}	Large	14.4	14.4	17.28
Typewriter	\texttt{...}	LARGE	17.28	17.28	20.74
Super^{script}	^{...}	huge	20.74	20.74	24.88
Sub$_{script}$	\textsubscript{...}	Huge	24.88	24.88	24.88

Table 3.1: Style and Size [1]

3.3   Colors

In LaTeX, colors can be set for text, tables, as well as background of a page. `color` package should be included so as to use basic colors like 'red', 'blue', 'green', 'white', 'black', 'yellow', 'cyan', and 'magenta', etc..

```
\usepackage{color}
```

Apart from these basic colors, one can use more colors mentioned in **dvipsnames** using the package **xcolor**. Some examples are 'Apricot', 'DarkOrchid', 'Thistle', 'OliveGreen', etc.. More colors can be found at [8].

```
\usepackage[dvipsnames]{xcolor}
```

The following syntax is used to change the color of text.

```
\textcolor{<Color>}{...text...}
\textcolor{<Color>!<percentage>}{..text..}
```

`\textcolor{Plum}` `{Pure Plum Color}`	Pure Plum Color
`\textcolor{Plum!70}` `{70% Plum 30% White}`	70% Plum 30% White
`\textcolor{Plum!60!Magenta}` `{60% Plum 40% Magenta}`	60% Plum 40% Magenta

The following syntax is used to change the background color of a page. Section 4.4 discusses coloring of tables.

```
\pagecolor{<ColorName>}
```

3.4   Text Alignment

By default the text is justified(i.e. left and right aligned). The following commands are used to align the text as left, right, or center.

Left Align	Right Align	Center Align
`\begin{flushleft}`	`\begin{flushright}`	`\begin{center}`
. . .	. . .	. . .
`\end{flushleft}`	`\end{flushright}`	`\end{center}`

3.5   Spacing

`setspace` package is used to increase/decrease the line spacing in the document.

```
\usepackage{setspace}
```

3.5.1   Fixed Line/Text Spacing

A document can have single spacing, one and a half spacing, double spacing, or custom spacing. The following commands change the spacing of entire document.

```
\singlespacing   OR
\onehalfspacing  OR
\doublespacing
```

The following example changes the spacing of a particular part.

```
\begin{singlespace | onehalfspace |
   doublespace}
...
\end{singlespace | onehalfspace |
   doublespace}
```

3.5.2 Custom Line/Text Spacing

Custom spacing is set as shown below.

```
Entire Document:
     \spacing{X} % X denotes a number
Part of Document:
     \begin{spacing}{X}
              ...
     \end{spacing}
```

3.5.3 Titles

titlespacing command is used to change the default spacing set for chapter, section, subsection, etc..

```
\usepackage{titlesec}
\titlespacing{chapter|section|subsection|
   subsubsection|paragraph}{<Left>}{<
   Before>}{<After>}
```

1. Left: Denotes the spacing from the left, in points

2. Before: Denotes the vertical space before the title, in points

3. After: Denotes the vertical space after the title, in points

The following example indents all subsections by 10pt, adds 30pt space before the title, and 15pt space after the title

```
\titlespacing*{\subsection}
              {10pt}{30pt}{15pt}
```

The following example indents all chapters by 10pt, reduce 50pt space before the title, and adds 20pt space after the title.

```
\titlespacing*{\chapter}
              {10pt}{-50pt}{20pt}
% Note: For chapters, you need to use
% \titleformat too.
```

Titleformat

```
\titleformat{chapter|section|subsection|
    subsubsection|paragraph}[display]
    {<format>}{<label>}{<sep>}
    {<before-code>}[<after-code>]
```

E.g.

```
\titleformat{\chapter}[display]{\huge\
    bfseries}{\chaptertitlename \ \
    thechapter}{10pt}{\Huge}
```

3.6 Bullets and Numbering

Style	Description	Commands
Itemize	Creates un-ordered / bullet lists.	`\begin{itemize}` `\item ...` `\item ...` `\end{itemize}`
Enumerate	Creates ordered/numbered lists. By default these are numbered as 1, 2, etc..	`\begin{enumerate}` `\item ...` `\item ...` `\end{enumerate}`
	To change this numbering to alphabetical or roman, do the following.	`\usepackage{` `enumerate}` `\begin{enumerate}` `[A.] Or` `\begin{enumerate}` `[i.]`
Description	A type of list (similar to the one given above). The difference is that there is no number or bullet associated with a point. Rather it contains a label (in bold font) followed by some description.	`\begin{description}` `\item[...] ...` `\item[...] ...` `\end{description}`

Table 3.2: Bullets and Numbering

3.7 Post script fonts

`pifont` package [10] is used to display post script fonts and zapf dingbats. Each number is associated with a character (from 33 to 254). Some examples are (☎, 37), (✎, 48), (✔, 52), etc.

3.7.1 Single, Fill, and Line

```
\ding{45}

\dingfill{161}

\dingline{168}
```

3.7.2 List

➤ Creates a list

➤ using dingbat

  ✌ can nest

➤ its dinglist

```
\begin{dinglist}{248}
   \item Creates a list
   \item using dingbat
   \begin{dinglist}{44}
      \item can nest
   \end{dinglist}
   \item its dinglist
\end{dinglist}
```

3.7.3 Auto List

❶ auto generated

❷ symbols change

  ✌ watch the

  ✎ difference

❸ its dingautolist

```
\begin{dingautolist}{202}
   \item auto generated
   \item symbols change
   \begin{dingautolist}{44}
      \item watch the
      \item difference
   \end{dingautolist}
   \item its dingautolist
\end{dingautolist}
```

3.8 Typesetting

3.8.1 Listings (Source Code - Programming)

lstlisting environment is used to display code in the document. listings package should be included. [11]

```
\usepackage{listings}
```

Writing Code in Document

```
\begin{lstlisting} ... \ end{lstlisting}
```

Loading from a file

lstinputlisting command is used to include code/text directly from the file, without explicitly writing it in the document.

```
\lstinputlisting[language=c++|python|...]
                {Filename.extension}
```

Formatting Source Code

lstdefinestyle is used to format the code using various attributes like backgroundcolor, frame, etc. Given below is one such example. A detailed explanation follows the example.

```
1  #include<iostream>
2  using namespace std;
3  //Function to add two numbers
4  int add(int num1, int num2) {
5      int answer;
6      answer = num1 + num2;
7      return answer;
8  }
9
10 int main() {
11     int num1, num2, result;
12     cout << "Enter two numbers \n";
13     cin >> num1 >> num2;
14     //Call the function 'add'
15     result = add(num1, num2);
16     cout << "Addition of " << num1 << " and " << num2
            << " is " << result;
17     return 0;
18 }
```

```
\lstdefinestyle{customc}{..Attributes..}
\lstset{style=customc}
```

Attributes	Description
`backgroundcolor=` `\color{Gray!20},`	sets gray background color
`frame=single,`	Adds a border to the code
`breaklines=true,`	wrap the text if the number of characters exceeds on a line. Does not wrap if it is set to false.
`xleftmargin=15pt,`	Sets 15pt as left margin
`language=c++,`	C++ language is set for the code. Other languages: Python, C, etc.
`showstringspaces=false,`	stringspaces, if set to true displays a space bar character instead of a space
`stepnumber=1,`	interval between two line-numbers.
`basicstyle=\normalsize` `\ttfamily`	Overall text in the code will be of default font size and ttfamily font face
`keywordstyle=\bfseries` `\color{OliveGreen},`	Keywords will be displayed in bold and OliveGreen color
`commentstyle=\itshape` `\color{Plum},`	Comments will be displayed in italics and Plum color
`identifierstyle=` `\color{blue},`	Identifiers will be displayed in blue
`stringstyle=\color{red},`	Strings will be displayed in red color
`numbers=left,`	Line numbers will be displayed on the left of the code. They can also be displayed on the right. Value as none will not display line numbers.
`numbersep=9pt,`	The space between the line number and the code will be 9pts
`numberstyle=\scriptsize` `\color{BrickRed},`	The line numbers will be displayed in scriptsize font size and BrickRed color

Table 3.3: Attributes in lstdefinestyle

3.8.2   Mathematics

LaTeX displays mathematics in a very systematic way. In simple words, it looks beautiful! Using some commands one can write simple to complex mathematical expressions without having to worry about how it gets displayed in the document. It renders the way a writer/reader would like to have it. `mathtools` package needs to be included. For more information refer [12]

```
\usepackage{mathtools}
```

Mathematics needs to be written between `$ and $` so as to distinguish between the normal text and mathematics text.

Simple Expressions and Brackets

Given below are some examples of simple mathematical expressions with it's equivalent LaTeX commands.

Examples	LaTeX Code
$(a+b)^2 = a^2 + 2ab + b^2$	`$(a+b)^2=a^2+2ab+b^2$`
$cos(2\theta) = 1 - 2sin^2\theta$	`$cos(2\theta)=1-2sin^2` `\theta$`
$c = a_1 \times b_1$	`$c = a_1 \times b_1 $`
$\sqrt{16} = 4$	`$\sqrt{16} = 4$`
$\sqrt[3]{64} = 4$	`$\sqrt[3]{64} = 4$`
$A \in B \ne \phi$	`$A \in B \ne \phi$`

Braces i.e. round, box, curly, etc., are used quite often in the expressions. They are very important as they convey how the expression will be computed. Consider the following example.

$$\{A + (B - [(C * D)/E])\}$$

This shows that C and D will be multiplied first which will then be divided by E, and so on. The braces over here are conveying the order of computation, but all are of the same size. The commands given below are used to increase the size of brackets.

```
$  \big (   ...     \big )    $
$  \Big (   ...     \Big )    $
$  \bigg (  ...    \bigg )  $
$  \Bigg (  ...    \Bigg )  $
```

Note: The round brackets in the commands given above can be replaced with box or curly.

Consider the modified example.

$$\left\{ A + \left(B - \left[(C \times D)/E \right] \right) \right\}$$

The syntax is as follows:

```
$ \Bigg\{ A+ \bigg ( B - \Big [ \big ( C
  \times D \big) / E \Big] \bigg) \Bigg\} $
```

Fractions

\frac command defines fractions. The syntax is as follows:

```
\frac{numerator}{denominator}
```

The numerator or the denominator can also be a fraction, which is also written using the frac command. Some examples and their corresponding LaTeXcodes are given below:

Examples	**LaTeX Code**
$\frac{A}{B} + \frac{C}{D} = 1$	`$\frac{A}{B}+\frac{C}{D}=1$`
$x = \frac{-b \pm \sqrt{b^2 - 4ac}}{2a}$	`$x = \frac{-b \pm` `\sqrt{b^2-4ac}}{2a}$`
$\frac{1}{10} + \frac{1}{8} \cdots + \frac{1}{2} \ge 4$	`$\frac{1}{10} + \frac{1}{8}` `\cdots + \frac{1}{2} \ge 4 $`
$\frac{2+3}{\frac{2}{4}} = 5 \times \frac{4}{2} = 10$	`$\frac{2+3}{\frac{2}{4}} = 5` `\times \frac{4}{2} = 10 $`

Equations

Equations are embedded between the begin and end of the equation environment. Only one equation can be written in it.

```
\begin{equation}
...
\end{equation}
```

It is center aligned with numbering on the extreme right and is numbered by default. The command **nonumber** is used so that the equation is not numbered.

Examples	LaTeX Code

$(a + b)(a - b) = a^2 - b^2$ (3.1)	```\begin{equation}```
	```(a+b)(a-b)=a^2-b^2```
	```\end{equation}```

$a + b \times c$ (3.2)	```\begin{equation}```
	```a + b \times c```
	```\end{equation}```

Unlike **equation** environment, the **align** environment is used for writing equations on multiple lines. & specifies the alignment point of the equation while \\ is used to specify the end of line.

$3x - 6 = 9$ (3.3)
 	
$3x = 9 + 6$
 	
$x = \dfrac{9 + 6}{3}$
 	
$x = 5$
	```\begin{align}```
	```3x - 6 &= 9 \\```
	```3x &= 9+6 \nonumber```
	```\\```
	```x &= \frac{9+6}{3}```
	```\nonumber \\```
	```x &= 5 \nonumber```
	```\end{align}```

`cases` environment is used to specify constraints and conditions. It is very similar to the `align` environment. An example is given below.

$$
f(x) = \begin{cases}
0 & \text{if } i = j, \\
x \text{ is even} & \text{if } x \in E \\
x/7 & \text{if } x \notin E \\
\infty & \text{if } x \ne 70
\end{cases}
$$

```
$ f(x) =
\begin{cases}
\text{0} &
    \text{if i=j,} \\
\text{x is even} &
    \text{if x
        $\in$E}\\
\text{x/7} &
 \text{if x
        $\notin$E}\\
\text{$\infty$} &
    \text{if x
        $\ne$70}\\
\end{cases} $
```

Matrix

Matrices are represented using the following environments:

Environment	A matrix
`matrix`	without border
`pmatrix`	with round bracket
`bmatrix`	with box bracket
`Bmatrix`	with curly bracket
`vmatrix`	with | as bracket style
`Vmatrix`	with || as bracket style

Note: The alignment of the numbers in the matrix are centered by default. The environment name followed by a * is used to change the alignment to left or right. The alignment 'l' i.e. left or 'r' i.e. right is mentioned in the box bracket. The syntax is shown below.

```
\begin{matrix*}[l|r]
  ...
\end{matrix*}
```

Given below are two examples of matrices.

$$\begin{pmatrix} 1 & 2 \\ 23 & 67 \end{pmatrix} + \begin{pmatrix} 4 & 5678 \\ 232 & 42 \end{pmatrix}$$

```
$ \begin{pmatrix}
1 & 2 \\ 23 & 67 \\
\end{pmatrix}
+   \begin{pmatrix}
4 & 5678 \\ 232 &
   42 \\
\end{pmatrix} $
```

$$\begin{Bmatrix} 1 & 2 \\ 23 & 67 \end{Bmatrix} + \begin{Bmatrix} 4 & 5678 \\ 232 & 42 \end{Bmatrix}$$

```
$ \begin{Bmatrix*}
    [r]
1 & 2 \\ 23 & 67 \\
   \end{Bmatrix*}
+ \begin{Bmatrix*}
    [r]
4 & 5678 \\ 232 &
   42 \\
\end{Bmatrix*} $
```

Summation

sum command is used to denote summation. The limits are specified using '^' and '_'. The syntax is given below.

```
\sum_{lower-limit}^{upper-limit}
```

Consider an example to sum values from -5 to 5 and store in variable ans.

$$\sum_{i=-5}^{5} ans = ans + i$$

```
$\sum_{i=-5}^{5} ans =
              ans + i$
```

$$\sum_{i=-5}^{5} ans = ans + i$$

```
$\displaystyle\sum_{i=-5}
            ^{5} ans = ans + i$
```

Integration

`int` command is used to denote integration. Similar to summation, the limits are also specified using '^' and '_'. Some examples are given below.

$$\int_a^b f(x)\mathrm{d}x$$

```
$ \displaystyle\int_{a}^
        {b} f(x) \mathrm{d}x $
```

$$\iint_R f(x,y)\mathrm{d}A$$

```
$ \displaystyle\iint_{R}
        f(x,y) \mathrm{d}A $
```

$$\int_a^b \left[\int_a^b f(x,y)\mathrm{d}y \right]\mathrm{d}x$$

```
$ \displaystyle\int_{a}^{b}
        \Big[ \int_{a}^{b} f(x,y)
        \mathrm{d}y \Big]
        \mathrm{d}x $
```

$$\int_0^\infty \frac{dx}{(x+1)\sqrt{x}} = \pi$$

```
$ \displaystyle\int_{0}^
        {\infty} \frac{dx}{(x+1)
        \sqrt{x}} = \pi $
```

$$\lim_{z \to a} \int_z^b f(x)dx$$

```
$\displaystyle\lim_{z\to a}
        \int_{z}^{b} f(x) dx$
```

3.9 Exercises

1. If I want my document to have 10pt font size, do I need to explicitly mention it? If yes, where?

2. Create a document and experiment with different font sizes, attributes, and colors

3. Create the following list as given below:

   - Tables

     (a) Basic structure
     (b) Borders
     (c) Spacing

   - Images

     (a) Sizing and scaling
     (b) Crop and rotate

4. Write LATEXcode for fourier series of a function f(x) as shown below

$$f(x) = \tfrac{1}{2}a_0 + \sum_{n=1}^{\infty} a_n cos(n\ x) + \sum_{n=1}^{\infty} b_n sin(n\ x)$$

   where

$$a_0 = \tfrac{1}{\pi} \int_{-\pi}^{\pi} f(x)dx$$

$$a_n = \tfrac{1}{\pi} \int_{-\pi}^{\pi} f(x)cos(n\ x)dx$$

$$b_n = \tfrac{1}{\pi} \int_{-\pi}^{\pi} f(x)sin(n\ x)dx$$

What you can do

1. Use correct punctuation marks like the hyphen, em-dash, en-dash, etc.

2. Specify font size for the document.

3. Set font size for certain part in the document.

4. Use different text attributes like bold, italics, etc.

5. Specify colors for text and page.

6. Align text: left, center, right.

7. Set vertical spacing between sections and paragraphs.

8. Specify points using bullets, numbering, and description.

9. Use different PostScript fonts for better visualization using `ding` command.

10. Display code in a well-formatted way using `lstlisting`.

11. Write various mathematical equations using `mathtools`.

Chapter 4
Tables

What you will learn

4.1   Basic Structure and Examples

LaTeX provides a tabular environment for creating tables. The basic structure of a table is given below:

```
\begin{tabular}{<Columns>}
   ...
\end{tabular}
```

The value of Columns is either 'l', 'r', 'c', or 'p{Xcm}'.

Columns	Denotes a column with
l	left alignment
c	center alignment
r	right alignment
p{Xcm}	left alignment whose width is X cm

Table 4.1: Columns of a table

The column width for columns created using either 'l', 'r', or 'c' depends on the size of the text in the column cell. The total count of these values denotes the number of columns in the table. The placement of | separates the column by a vertical line.

Consider the following example that creates a table with 4 columns. The alignment of first 3 columns is center, left, and right respectively. The last column is left aligned but has column width of 1 cm.

```
\begin{tabular}{||c|lr|p{1cm}||}
   ...
\end{tabular}
```

While creating the content of the table, note the following:

- Columns are separated using &

- Place \\ to denote end of the row

- \hline places a horizontal line

- \cline{i-j} places a horizontal line from column i to j

- \newline places new-line within a cell (if p{Xcm} is used)

4.1.1 Basic Table

No.	Name	Stream
1	Sheetal	CS
2	Jeet	EE
3	Priyanka	CS

```
\begin{tabular}{clr}
No. & Name & Stream
  \\
1 & Sheetal & CS \\
2 & Jeet & EE \\
3 & Priyanka & CS \\
\end{tabular}
```

4.1.2 Table with border

No.	Name	Stream
1	Sheetal	CS
2	Jeet	EE
3	Priyanka	CS

```
\begin{tabular}
        {|c|l|l|}
\hline
No.& Name & Stream\\
\hline
\hline
1 & Sheetal & CS \\
\hline
2 & Jeet & EE \\
\hline
3 & Priyanka & CS\\
\hline
\end{tabular}
```

4.1.3   Table with Fixed Column Width

No.	Name	Stream
1	Sheetal	CS
2	Jeet	EE

```
\begin{tabular}
   {|p{1cm}|p{5cm}|r|}
\hline
No.& Name & Stream\\
\hline
1 & Sheetal & CS \\
\hline
2 & Jeet & EE \\
\hline \end{tabular}
```

Note: It is a good practice of using only horizontal lines and avoid using vertical lines in a table. It makes the table look less cluttered and neat. The vertical lines used in the book are only for illustration purpose.

4.1.4   Table with Borders (cline)

R1-C1	R1-C2	R1-C3
R2-C1	R2-C2	R2-C3
R3-C1	R3-C2	R3-C3

```
\begin{tabular}{ccc}
\hline
R1-C1 & R1-C2 &
        R1-C3 \\
\cline{1-2}
R2-C1 & R2-C2 &
        R2-C3 \\
\cline{2-3}
R3-C1 & R3-C2 &
        R3-C3 \\
\hline
\end{tabular}
```

4.1.5   Spacing in Tables

The space inside the table cell is specified using the 'arraystretch' command as shown below. By default this value is set to 1.

No.	Name	Stream
1	Sheetal	CS
2	Jeet	EE

```
\renewcommand{\
    arraystretch}{2}
\begin{tabular}{clr}
\hline
No.& Name & Stream\\
\hline ... \hline
\end{tabular}
```

4.1.6   Table with Dashed Borders

arydshln package [13] is used to create horizontal and vertical dashed lines. Instead of | for creating a vertical line use ':'. The syntax for creating horizontal dashed lines is

```
\hdashline[<dash size>/
          <space between dashes>]
```

R1-C1	R1-C2	R1-C3
R2-C1	R2-C2	R2-C3
R3-C1	R3-C2	R3-C3

```
\begin{tabular}
        {:c:c:c:}
\hdashline[1pt/5pt]
R1-C1 & R1-C2 &
        R1-C3 \\
\cdashline{1-1}[5pt
    /5pt]
R2-C1 & R2-C2 &
        R2-C3 \\
\cdashline{3-3}[3pt
    /7pt]
R3-C1 & R3-C2 &
        R3-C3 \\
\hdashline[1pt/5pt]
\end{tabular}
```

In the example given above, the outermost horizontal line of the table is of size 1pt and spacing of 5pt. The line separating R1-C1 and R2-C1 is of size 5pt and spacing of 5pt, whereas the line separating R2-C3 is of size 3pt and spacing of 7pt.

4.2   Merge Columns

`multicolumn` command is used to merge columns.

```
\multicolumn{<TotalColumns>}
        {<Alignment>}{<Text>}
```

List of Students		
No.	Name	Stream
1	Sheetal K	CS
2	Jeet	EE
	Class Avg	7.33

```
\begin{tabular}
        {|l|l|l|l|}
\hline
\multicolumn{3}
    {|c|}{List of
        Students} \\
\hline
No.& Name & Stream\\
\hline
1 & Sheetal & CS \\
\hline
2 & Jeet & EE \\
\hline
\multicolumn{2}
    {|r|}{Class Avg} &
        7.33 \\
\hline
\end{tabular}
```

4.3   Merge Rows

Unlike merging columns of a table, merging rows require `multirow` package.

```
\usepackage{multirow}
\multirow{<NumberOfRows>}{<Width>}
        {<Text>}
```

The width can be specified as Xcm or as *. * denotes width of the content.

Grp.	Name	Marks
	Sheetal	8
A	Jeet	9
	Jyoti	5
	Priyanka	5
B	Neel	9

```
\begin{tabular}
    {|c|l|r|}
\hline
Grp.& Name & Marks\\
\hline
\multirow{3}{*}{A} &
    Sheetal & 8 \\
& Jeet & 9 \\
& Jyoti & 5\\
\hline
\multirow{2}{*}{B} &
    Priyanka & 5\\
& Neel & 9\\
\hline
\end{tabular}
```

4.4 Table Color

4.4.1 Column, Row, and Cell

`colortbl` package is used to color the columns, rows, and cells.

No.	Name	Stream
1	Sheetal	CS
2	Jeet	EE
3	Priyanka	CS

```
\begin{tabular}
    {>{\columncolor
        {blue!20}}cll}
No.& Name & Stream\\
\rowcolor{green!30}
1 & Sheetal & CS \\
2 & Jeet & EE \\
3 & Priyanka &
    \cellcolor{red!40}
        CS\\
\end{tabular}
```

Type	Syntax	Description
Row	\rowcolor{color!percentage} E.g. \rowcolor{green!30}	Colors entire row. Should be written before the row begins
Column	>{\columncolor{color!percentage}} E.g. >{\columncolor{blue!20}}	Colors entire column. Should be written while defining columns
Cell	\cellcolor{color!percentage} E.g. \cellcolor{red!40}	Colors only the cell. Should be written before the text in that cell

4.4.2   Alternate Rows

Different colors are applied to alternate rows of a table using \rowcolors command. The syntax is given below.

```
\rowcolors{<Starting row number>}
   {<Odd row color>}{<Even row color>}
```

The following example creates a table with alternate row colors of lavender and cornflowerblue.

No.	Name	Stream
1	Sheetal	CS
2	Jeet	EE
3	Priyanka	CS
4	Ajit	CS

```
\rowcolors{1}
{Lavender!50}
{CornflowerBlue!50}
\begin{tabular}{cll}
\hline
No. & Name & Stream
   \\
...
\end{tabular}
```

4.5   Long table

Tables that extend beyond one page do not get displayed. For such tables, instead of `tabular`, `longtable` environment needs to be used. Rest of the commands remain same.

```
\usepackage{longtable}
\begin{longtable}...
...
\end{longtable}
```

`endhead` command is used to repeat row(s) i.e. headers of the table on every page

```
\begin{longtable}{cll}
\hline
No. & Name & Stream \\
\hline
\endhead
1 & Sheetal & CS \\
2 & Jeet & EE \\
...
100 & Raj & ME \\
\hline
\end{longtable}
```

4.6   Table Environment

The table environment is used to position the table in the document and to specify the caption of the table.

```
\begin{table}[position]
\begin{tabular}
...
\end{tabular}
\caption{...}
\end{table}
```

Position	Place the table
h	approximately here
t	at the top of the page
b	at the bottom of the page
H	exactly here

Table 4.2: Position Table

4.7 Exercises

Create tables similar to the ones given below:

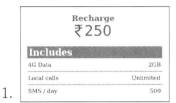

1.

Historical population		
Year	Pop.	±%
1861	194,500	—
1871	212,432	+9.2%
1881	273,952	+29.0%
1901	422,411	+54.2%
1911	518,917	+22.8%
1921	660,235	+27.2%
1931	930,926	+41.0%
1936	1,150,589	+23.6%
1951	1,651,754	+43.6%
1961	2,188,160	+32.5%
1971	2,781,993	+27.1%
1981	2,840,259	+2.1%
1991	2,775,250	−2.3%
2001	2,663,182	−4.0%
2011	2,617,175	−1.7%
2017	2,876,051	+9.9%
Source: ISTAT, 2001		

2.

Climate data for Rome Ciampino Airport (altitude: 105 m sl, 13 km (8 mi) south-east from Colosseum, $\star$ satellite view)													[hide]
Month	Jan	Feb	Mar	Apr	May	Jun	Jul	Aug	Sep	Oct	Nov	Dec	Year
Average high °C (°F)	11.9 (53.4)	13.0 (55.4)	15.2 (59.4)	17.7 (63.9)	22.5 (73)	26.5 (80.5)	30.0 (86)	29.8 (85.6)	26.5 (79.7)	21.4 (70.5)	15.9 (60.6)	12.6 (54.7)	20.4 (68.7)
Daily mean °C (°F)	7.5 (45.5)	8.7 (46.9)	10.2 (50.4)	12.6 (54.7)	17.2 (63)	21.1 (70)	24.1 (75.4)	24.5 (76.1)	21.1 (70)	16.6 (61.9)	11.4 (52.6)	8.4 (47.1)	15.2 (59.4)
Average low °C (°F)	3.1 (37.6)	3.5 (38.3)	5.2 (41.4)	7.5 (45.5)	11.6 (52.9)	15.3 (59.5)	18.0 (64.4)	18.5 (65.3)	15.2 (59.4)	11.3 (52.3)	6.9 (44.4)	4.2 (39.6)	10.0 (50)
Average precipitation mm (inches)	66.9 (2.634)	73.3 (2.886)	57.8 (2.276)	80.5 (3.169)	52.8 (2.079)	34.0 (1.339)	19.2 (0.756)	36.9 (1.449)	73.3 (2.886)	113.3 (4.461)	115.4 (4.543)	81.0 (3.189)	804.3 (31.665)
Average precipitation days (≥ 1 mm)	7.8	7.6	7.5	9.2	6.2	4.3	2.1	3.3	6.5	8.2	9.7	6.9	79.4
Mean monthly sunshine hours	120.9	132.4	167.4	201.0	263.5	296.0	331.7	297.6	237.0	195.3	129.0	111.6	2,472.8
Source: Servizio Meteorologico,[3][4] data of sunshine hours[5] (1971–2000)													

3.

Note: The tables for exercises 2 and 3 are taken for only illustration purpose from `https://en.wikipedia.org/wiki/Rome`

What you can do

1. Create a table: basic, with and without border (dashed vs normal).

2. Specify the column width of the table.

3. Merge columns and rows.

4. Add colors to a cell, row, column, or entire table.

5. Add alternate coloring to rows.

6. Deal with long tables with header rows repeating on every page.

7. Position tables in the document.

8. Add captions to the table.

Chapter 5
Images

What you will learn

LaTeX makes use of the **graphicx** package to insert figures in a document. This chapter presumes that .pdf document is being created from .tex, using **pdflatex** command. To know more visit [14]. The following image file extentions are supported: **.png**, **.jpg**, **.pdf**, **.eps**. Note that .pdf file can also be included using image commands.

graphicx package is used along with `includegraphics` command to insert an image in the document.

```
\usepackage{graphicx}
\includegraphics[Attribute1,Attribute2,..]
                {FileName.extention}
```

5.1   Image Size

`width` and `height` attributes are used to set the size of the image.

```
\includegraphics
   [width=X<unit>]
   {flower.png}
OR
\includegraphics
   [height=X<unit>]
   {flower.png}
```

X denotes the size, while <unit> denotes the dimensions in centimeter, inches, etc..

Specifying only the height or width scales the image by maintaining the aspect ratio accordingly. E.g.

```
\includegraphics
   [height=2cm]
   {flower.png}
```

5.2   Scaling an Image

The attribute `scale` is used to scale an image, without explicitly specifying the size in height or width.

```
% Scales the image by a factor of X
\includegraphics[scale=X]{flower.png}

%E.g. 1 - Scales (reduces) by half
\includegraphics[scale=0.5]{flower.png}

%E.g. 2 - Scales (doubles) the image
\includegraphics[scale=2]{flower.png}
```

5.3 Trim/Crop Image

An image can be cropped from all four sides. The attribute, `clip` should be set to `true`, and the attribute `trim` should specify the values and units in the order (left, bottom, right, and top). The following example crops left by 2mm, bottom by 3mm, right by 4mm, and top by 10mm.

```
\includegraphics[clip=true, trim=2mm 3mm
                 4mm 1mm]{flower.png}
```

5.4 Rotate Image

The attribute `angle` is used to rotate an image (in degrees).

```
% Rotates image
% by 45 degrees
\includegraphics
   [angle=45]
   {flower.png}
```

5.5 Border

`fbox` command is used to set image borders.

```
\fbox
{\includegraphics{flower.jpg}}
```

5.5.1 Border Thickness

The command, `setlength`, along with `fboxrule` specifies the thickness of border.

```
%Border thickness is 2pt
\setlength\fboxrule{2pt}
\fbox
{\includegraphics{flower.png}}
```

5.5.2   Space between border and image

The command, `setlength`, along with `fboxsep` is used to specify the space between border and image.

```
\setlength\fboxsep{15pt}
\fbox{\includegraphics{flower.png}}
```

5.6   Use as Figures

The `figure` environment is used to insert images at a specified position in a document and is also used to specify the caption of the image.

```
\begin{figure}[position]
        \includegraphics ...
        \caption{Caption of the image}
\end{figure}
```

Position	Place the image
h	approximately here
t	at the top of the page
b	at the bottom of the page
H	exactly here. At the same location as in the .tex file
p	on a special page
!	override internal parameters

Table 5.1: Position Images

```
\begin{figure}[h]
   \begin{center}
      \includegraphics[scale=1.4]{pen.png}
      \caption{Pen}
   \end{center}
\end{figure}
```

\listoffigures is used to display the caption of all the images. This command is usually written after the table of contents.

5.7 Wrap Figures

There are certain situations when it is needed to place the image and text side by side, for example, an image on the left with its appropriate description on the right. This can be achieved using the two methods given below:

5.7.1 Wrapfigure Environment

The wrapfigure environment is one of the methods for positioning images with text.

```
\usepackage{wrapfig}
\begin{wrapfigure}{l|L|r|R|i|I|o|O}{width}
   \includegraphics ...
   \caption{Flower}
\end{wrapfigure}
```

- l and L: Denotes image on the left and text on the right

- r and R: Denotes image on the right and text on the left

- i and I: Inside edge

- o and I: Away from binding

Note: The lowercase implies the image to be placed exactly here, while upper case means that the image can float.

Example 1

```
\begin{wrapfigure}{R}{0.2\textwidth}
   \includegraphics[width=1in]{lilies.jpg}
   \caption{Flower}
\end{wrapfigure}
\paragraph{}
The great variety of delicate ...
```

The great variety of delicate and beautiful flowers has inspired the works of numerous poets, especially from the 18th-19th century Romantic era. Famous examples include William Wordsworth's I Wandered Lonely as a Cloud and William Blake's Ah! Sun-Flower. Because of their varied and colorful appearance, flowers ...

Figure 5.1: Right Align

Example 2

```
\begin{wrapfigure}{l}{0.5\textwidth}
 \includegraphics[width=1.5in]{lilies.jpg}
 \caption{Flower}
\end{wrapfigure}
\paragraph{} The great variety of  ...
```

Figure 5.2: Left aligned

The great variety of delicate and beautiful flowers has inspired the works of numerous poets, especially from the 18th-19th century Romantic era. Famous examples include William Wordsworth's I Wandered Lonely as a Cloud and William Blake's Ah! ...

5.7.2 Figwindow using picinpar Package

Another way of inserting images alongside a paragraph is by using `picinpar` package.

```
\usepackage{picinpar}
\begin{figwindow}[<No. of lines>,l|r|c,
      <code to insert image>,{<caption>}]
Paragraph text ....
\end{figwindow}
```

- No. of lines: Specifies the number of lines that need to be skipped from the top before displaying the image

- l or r or c: Denotes whether the image should be left, right, or center aligned

- Code to insert image: Mentions the includegraphics command along with its attributes to insert the image

- Caption: The caption of an image

- Paragraph text: The paragraph that you need to display alongside the image

Example 1 - Left Aligned and skipping 3 lines

```
\begin{figwindow} [3, l,
      \includegraphics[width=1.1in]{flower
         .jpg},
      {left align + 3 lines skipped}]
      Flowers provide less food than other
         ...
\end{figwindow}
```

Flowers provide less food than other major plants parts (seeds, fruits, roots, stems and leaves) but they provide several important foods and spices. Flower vegetables include broccoli, cauliflower  and artichoke. The most expensive spice, saffron, consists of dried stigmas of a crocus. Other flower spices are cloves and capers. Hops flowers are used to flavor beer. Marigold flowers are fed to chickens to give their egg yolks a golden yellow color, which consumers find more desirable; **Figure** **5.3:** left align + 3 lines skipped dried and ground marigold flowers are also used as a spice and colouring agent in Georgiancuisine. Flowers of the dandelion and elder are often made into wine. Bee pollen, pollen collected from bees, is considered a health food by some people.

Example 2 - Right Aligned and skipping 0 lines

```
\begin{figwindow}  [0,  r,
      \includegraphics[width=1.1in]{lilies
          .jpg},
      {Right  align  +  0  lines  skipped}]
      Flowers  provide  less  food  than  other
             . . .
\end{figwindow}
```

Flowers provide less food than other major plants parts (seeds, fruits, roots, stems and leaves) but they provide several important foods and spices. Flower vegetables include broccoli, cauliflower and artichoke. The most expensive spice, saffron, consists of dried stigmas of a crocus. Other flower spices are cloves and capers. Hops flowers are used to flavor beer. Marigold  **Figure 5.4:** Right align + 0 lines skipped flowers are fed to chickens to give their egg yolks a golden yellow color, which consumers find more desirable; dried and ground marigold flowers are also used as a spice and colouring ...

Example 3 - Center Aligned and skipping 2 lines

```
\begin{figwindow} [2, c,
      \includegraphics[width=1.1in]{lilies
         .jpg},
      {Center align + 2 lines skipped}]
      Flowers provide less food than other
         . . .
\end{figwindow}
```

Flowers provide less food than other major plants parts (seeds, fruits, roots, stems and leaves) but they provide several important foods and spices.  Flower vegetables include broccoli, cauliflower and artichoke. The most expensive spice, saffron, consists of dried stigmas of a crocus. Other flower spices are cloves and capers. Hops flowers are used to flavor beer. Marigold flowers are fed to chickens to give their egg yolks a golden yellow color, which consumers find more desirable; dried

Figure 5.5: Center align + 2 lines skipped

and ground marigold flowers are also used as a spice and colouring agent in Georgiancuisine. Flowers of the dandelion and elder are often made into wine. Bee pollen, pollen collected from bees, is considered a health food by some people.

Note: The image and text used in the 5 examples of this chapter are taken from Wikipedia and are only used for illustration purpose.

5.8   Exercises

1. Create a document that displays the weather of Mumbai city. You can take some random images of a cloud:

2. Display the FIFA World Cup 2018 final match score:

What you can do

1. Include an image.

2. Add border with variable thickness to it.

3. Resize the image by specifying width and height or by using scale factor.

4. Crop the image based on the specifications.

5. Rotate the image.

6. Add image as figures and get the list of figures with auto figure numbering and captions.

7. Display images along with text (side by side) using different ways.

Chapter 6
Include PDF files

What you will learn

LaTeX allows us to include some or all pages of a .pdf file into another document. **pdfpages** package is used for this purpose. [15]

```
\usepackage[final|draft|demo]{pdfpages}
```

Final: Default one. Inserts the .pdf file mentioned

Draft: Inserts a blank box with the filename instead of the .pdf

Demo: Inserts an empty blank page instead of the .pdf file

6.1   Insert all Pages

The following inserts all pages of a `.pdf` document.

```
\includepdf[pages=-]{Filename.pdf}
```

6.2   Insert Certain Pages

To insert specific pages, the attribute `pages` should have page numbers separated by a comma, while to insert a page range, the attribute `pages` should have the starting and ending page number separated by a hyphen. Curly braces { } are used to insert a blank page. The following command inserts page 1, page 3, a blank page, and pages 5 to 18 from the MOOC.pdf file.

```
\includepdf[pages={1,3,{},{5-18}}]
            {MOOC.pdf}
```

6.3   Page Style

`pagecommand` is used to set page style of pages in the `pdf` file. The command given below sets a plain page style to the MOOC.pdf file.

```
\includepdf[pages=-,pagecommand={
       \thispagestyle{plain}}]{MOOC.pdf}
```

This page style can be modified as desired. More page styles are mentioned in section 2.3.1.

6.4 Scale

The .pdf file which is to be included in the document can be scaled (increased or decreased) in the similar way a figure is, i.e. using the attribute `scale`. This was discussed in section 5.2

```
\includepdf[pages=-, scale=0.75]{MOOC.pdf}
```

6.5 Crop

The .pdf file which is to be included in the document can be cropped in the similar way a figure is, i.e. using two attributes `clip` and `trim`. This was discussed in section 5.3

```
\includepdf[pages=-, clip=true, trim=20mm
    10mm 10mm 20mm]{MOOC.pdf}
```

6.6 Rotate

The .pdf file which is to be included in the document can be rotated in the similar way a figure is, i.e. using the attribute `angle`. This was discussed in section 5.4.

```
\includepdf[pages=-, angle=90]{MOOC.pdf}
```

What you can do

1. Include all pages or some pages of a .pdf into the document.

2. Modify the page style.

3. Scale, crop, and rotate the included .pdf file.

Chapter 7
Title, Links, Citing

What you will learn

7.1   Make Title

The   maketitle
command inserts the
details provided in
the different tags like
'title', 'author', and
'date'.   These tags
were   discussed   in
section 1.3.2.

```
\title{Document title}
\author{Name 1 \\ Name 2}
\date{\today}
\begin{document}
...
\maketitle
...
\end{document}
```

7.2   Title Page

Apart   from   the
basic   information,
sometimes one needs
to   include   the   in-
stitute name, logo,
etc.. For this purpose
LaTeX   provides   us
with an environment
called titlepage.

```
\begin{document}
   \begin{titlepage}
      \begin{center}
         Info, Images, etc
      \end{center}
   \end{titlepage}
\end{document}
```

7.3   Hyperlinks

Hyperlinks in a document are created using hyperref package. All URLs, links, ToC, list of figures, list of tables, or any
cross-referencing will be hyperlinked (clickable). More information about customizing hyperlinks can be found here. [16]

```
\usepackage{hyperref}
```

URL: url command is used to create URLs. Note that the
entire link will be displayed in the document.

```
\url{https://firuza.github.io/}
```

href: Similar to url, it also creates links but does not display the entire link. Instead, it displays the alias that is provided.

```
\href{https://firuza.github.io/}{MyPage}
```

Note that, here instead of the entire link, only 'My Page' will be displayed in the document, but, if one clicks on My Page, the URL will load.

7.4 Cross-referencing

Cross referencing is referring to a content present in the document itself. LaTeX helps creating it, using `label` and `ref` commands. Page number is cross referenced using **pageref** command. Given below is an example.

Setting Labels
Section 2.3 Matrix

```
\label{sec:matrix}
...
...
```

Section 5.1 Structures

```
\begin{figure}
  \includegraphics
    {...}
  \caption{Types
    \label{fig:
      types}}
\end{figure}
```

Cross Referencing
Section 10.4 Recapitulate

```
Recall our
    discussion on
    matrix in section
     ~\ref{sec:matrix
    } on page
\pageref{sec:matrix}
...
...
As shown in the
    figure ~\ref{fig:
    types} on page
\pageref{fig:types}
    ...
```

7.5 References (Bibliography)

Creating a bibliography involves (a) .bib file, (b) citing the text in .tex file, (c) and finally compiling and building it, so that the bibliography is displayed in our document. The following three subsections describe the process.

7.5.1 Bib File (.bib)

References are written in a `.bib` file as given below

```
@misc{ KEY,
    author = { },
    title = {},
    month = {},
    year = {},
    url = ""
}
```

Note: Instead of 'misc' (miscellaneous), 'article', 'book', etc. i.e. other types of references, can also be mentioned.

7.5.2 Citing in .tex

The `url` package needs to be included and the bibliography style needs to be mentioned. Thereafter, `cite` command is used at appropriate place. At the end of the document, bibliography needs to be displayed.

```
\usepackage{url}
\bibliographystyle{abbrv|alpha|unsrt|acm}
...
\cite{KEY} %Here, KEY is what was given in
    .bib
...
\bibliography{Filename_of_.bib_file}
```

Note: `nocite` command is used to include the reference without being cited.

```
\nocite{KEY}
```

7.5.3 Compiling and Building

```
pdflatex filename.tex
bibtex filename %filename without .tex
pdflatex filename.tex
pdflatex filename.tex
```

7.6 Index

Index is nothing but a list of words and the page number on which they appear in the document. It is most commonly used in books for easy reference. It is usually displayed at the end of the book. They are created using `makeidx` package. `makeindex` command is used to enable indexing.

```
\usepackage{makeidx}
\makeindex
```

7.6.1 Creating Index Keys in .tex

`index` command is used to create index keys at appropriate place in the .tex file. The different types of keys and formatting are given in the table 7.1.

```
\index{key}
E.g. \index{flower}
```

7.6.2 Displaying Index

`printindex` command is then used to display the index in the document. This command is usually placed at the end of the document.

```
\printindex
```

Style	Description	Command
flower, 40	Default format for displaying index key & page number	\index{flower}
rose, 42	'rose' is a subentry of the parent 'rose'. It is indented	\index{flower!rose}
fruit, 56	The index key is formatted as bold	\index{fruit@ \textbf{fruit}}
vegetable, **58**	The page number is formatted as bold	\index{vegetable| textbf}
tulip, *see* flower	The key 'tulip' has a cross reference to key 'flower'	\index{tulip| see{flower}}

Table 7.1: Types and Formatting Index Keys

7.6.3 Compiling and Building

```
makeindex filename
pdflatex filename.tex
```

7.7   Exercises

1. What information does the command `maketitle` display?

2. Which command (a) `url` (b) `href`, should be used if the link has an alias?

3. Consider the statement: 'We have discussed the rotation of images in section 3 of this article'. The section number 3 should be hyperlinked such that it navigates to section 3 on clicking. Implement the same.

4. Highlight the process of creating an index.

What you can do

1. Create title page using `maketitle` command.

2. Create a custom title page.

3. Add hyperlinks and URLs to the document.

4. Use cross-referencing to reference text within the document.

5. Add references by creating a .bib file and citing them in the document.

6. Create and display index (back index).

Chapter 8
More for the road

What you will learn

Finally think larger !

This chapter covers some tips that one can follow while using LaTeX so as to produce better documents and avoid un-necessary hurdles (warnings and errors) while creating it.

8.1 Best Practices

✐ While writing large documents or books, create different (.tex) files and include them using `include` command in the main file. Example is given below.

mybook.tex	ch01.tex	ch02.tex
`% All Packages`	`\chapter`	`\chapter`
`\begin{document}`	`{...}`	`{...}`
`\include{ch01}`	`\section`	`\section`
`\include{ch02}`	`{...}`	`{...}`
`\end{document}`		

✐ Version Control and Collaboration

    ✐ There are many instances when one says:

    ✐ "My document produced successful results yesterday, but today something happened and I cannot figure out why this error is cropping up."

    ✐ "I need to collaborate with 10 people in my team to produce project report. I am unable to handle emails and collate them."

    ✐ This is where version control comes handy. One can also know what work is done and by whom, revert back to the desired stage, find out the differences, etc..

    ✐ There are various tools which one can use are: (i) Subversion (SVN) [17], (ii) GitHub [18], (iii) GitLab [19], (iv) Darcs [20], etc.

✐ Web based LaTeXeditors like Sharelatex [21], Overleaf [22], Verbosus [23], Papeeria [24], etc. are also available. Browse the wiki link [2] to get a list and comparison of LaTeXeditors (online and offline).

✍ Apart from the regular versioning tools which provide facility to find differences between two versions, the command `latexdiff` can also be used for this purpose. The syntax is as follows:

```
latexdiff 1.tex 2.tex > diff.tex
pdflatex diff.tex
```

The diff.pdf will highlight content which was added, deleted, or modified. For more information and options please see [25].

✍ Do not double quote character present on keyboard. Use ` for opening quotes and ' for closing quotes.

8.2 Types of files

When a .tex file is built, along with .pdf files some other files are also created. These are nothing but auxiliary files. The process is to (a) collect information from .tex, (b) create these auxiliary files, (c) use these auxiliary files and .tex to render the document (.pdf). These files are temporary and can be deleted, as they shall be created again. However, there are some files which are important and should not be deleted, such as (.cls, .sty, .bib, .tex).

① General

    ① **sty:** extends/modifies existing styling commands or adding a new feature. These are called in .tex file by `\usepackage` command.

    ② **tex:** File created by us

    ③ **aux:** Stores general information which is passed from previous build to the next one.

    ④ **log:** Gives the build report and reports errors, if any.

    ⑤ **out:** Stores all hyperrefs

⑥ **pdf**: The rendered document

② Entries and Lists

　① **toc**: Table of contents. This file is generatd by the command, `\tableofcontents`. So, when .tex file is built this file is first created which inturn is used to generate the actual table of contents in .pdf file.

　② **lot**: list of tables. It is generatd by `\listoftables` command. The process is similar to .toc file.

　③ **lof**: list of figures. It is generatd by the command, `\listoffigures`. The process is similar to .toc file.

③ Bibliography

　① **bib**: This file is created by us that contains our references.

　② **bbl**: This file contains the output of `bibtex` command, which is then used to LaTeXto generate bibliography.

　③ **blg**: This file contains the logs and errors (if any) of `bibtex`.

④ Index

　① **idx**: This file stores all the indexed words. This file is processed with `makeidx`

　② **ilg**: The log file generated while executing `makeidx` command

　③ **ind**: This is the processed .idx file. LaTeXuses this file to generate the index in .pdf file

8.3   Handling Errors

8.3.1   Introduction

While compiling, if LaTeXencounters text or commands which cannot be understood then it displays error messages. The most frequently occurred error messages are related to the syntax. For example, a missing bracket, spelling mistake in the commands, or a package is not included, etc.

8.3.2 Reading Error Messages

To resolve the errors encountered, it is very important to understand the error message. The format is as follows:

```
! <Error message >
l.<Line number > <immediate command >
```

8.3.3 Most Common Errors

Given below is the list and description of the most common errors one can encounter.

Missing curly brace in Environment

The following error message is displayed if a curly brace is missing for either 'begin' or 'end' of environment.

`\begin{center`	Runaway argument?
`hello`	{center hello \end {center}
`\end{center}`	! Paragraph ended before \begin was complete.
	<to be read again>
	\par
	l.13
	?

Environment not ended or Mismatch

This type of error occurs when the environment is not ended or is ended with another environment. LaTeX matches every `\begin` with `\end`. Hence, it displays an error message stating that the environment started with one but ended with another.

`\begin{center}`
`hello`
`OR`
`\begin{itemize}`
`\item one`
`\end{enumerate}`
	! LaTeX Error: \begin{center} on input line 30 ended by \end{document}.
	See the LaTeX manual or LaTeX Companion for explanation.
	Type H <return> for immediate help.
	...
	l.35 \end{document}

Unknown command

This type of error occurs when the command is not known to LaTeX or usually if there is some spelling mistake.

`\pagebreaks`	! Undefined control sequence. l.43 \pagebreaks

Mismatch in curly brace

This type of error occurs when the curly braces do not match. In the example given, there is one open curly brace while two closed curly braces.

`\textbf{hello}}`	! Too many }'s. <recently read> } l.48 \textbf{hello}}

The following example shows one open curly brace but no closed.

`\textbf{hello`	Runaway argument? {hello \par \par \par \end {document} \par ! File ended while scanning use of \textbf . <inserted text> \par < * > errors.tex

Missing item

This type of error occurs when items are not mentioned in the listing environment.

`\begin{itemize}` `\end{itemize}`	! LaTeX Error: Something's wrong– perhaps a missing \item. See the LaTeX manual or LaTeX Companion for explanation. Type H <return> for immediate help. ... l.101 \end{itemize}

Package not included

This type of error occurs when some command is used without including its respective package. The following error can be resolved by including `multicol package`.

`\begin` `{multicols}{2}` `column 1` `column 2` `\end{multicols}`	! LaTeX Error: Environment multicols undefined. See the LaTeX manual or LaTeX Companion for explanation. Type H <return> for immediate help. ... l.63 \begin{multicols} {2} ?

Style File not found

This error occurs when the style file is not found by LaTeX. To resolve this, one should either (a) install it (b) download it in the desired folder.

| `\usepackage`
`{multicols}` | ! LaTeX Error: File 'multicols.sty' not found.
Type X to quit or <RETURN> to proceed,
or enter new name. (Default extension: sty)
Enter file name: |

Errors in Tabular

Some errors that can occur in a tabular environment are missing of '&' and '\\'. The following error message is displayed.

```
! Extra alignment tab has been changed to
  \cr.
<recently read> \endtemplate
1.74     3 &
4
?
```

8.4 New commands and environment

Apart from the various commands and environment provided to us, there is sometimes a need to write new commands or environments or to re-define them. It is because that

✎ There is a LaTeXcommand which is used very frequently in the document and is too long.

✎ There is a need to enhance the command based on some requirements.

For more information please refer [26]

8.4.1 Commands

`newcommand` is used to redefine or write new commands. The syntax is as follows.

```
\newcommand <newCommandName >[<
   NumberOfArguments -Optional >]{
   ActualCommand}
```

Example 1: This example redefines the `textbf` command with a new command B. So, one would then write \B{text} to make the text bold.

```
\newcommand\B{\textbf}
```

Example 2: This example redefines the `hdashline` command with a new command `hd`. So, one would then write \hd to have a horizontal dashed line of 1pt/5pt.

```
\newcommand\hd{\hdashline[1pt/5pt]}
```

Example 3: This example creates a command 'discussion' which has one argument. This command will display the text 'This was discussed in section' along with the text as an argument. So, one would then write \discusison{5.2} to display 'This was discussed in section 5.2'.

```
\newcommand{\discussion}[1]{This was
   discussed in \textbf{section #1} }
```

Example 4: This example creates a new command called `cd` which also has one argument. This redefines the `cdashline` command with size of 3pt/7pt. So, one would then write \cd{1-3} where 1-3 denotes the column number in the table.

```
\newcommand{\cd}[1]{\cdashline{#1}[3pt/7
   pt] }
```

8.4.2   Environment

`newenvironment` is used to write new environment. The syntax is as follows.

```
\newenvironment{newEnvironmentName}
    [NumberOfArguments-Optional]
    {<CommandsBefore>}{<CommandsAfter>}
```

Commands specified in 'CommandsBefore' will execute when the new environment begins while the ones specified in 'CommandsAfter' will execute when the new environment ends. Consider an example where we need to decorate a text as shown below:

It would be great if it could be written by writing a 'decorate' environment

```
\begin{decorate} All the best ! \end{
    decorate}
```

It is possible by writing a new environment called 'decorate'

```
\newenvironment{decorate}
{ \huge \begin{center} \dingfill{87} \\ }
{ \\ \dingfill{96}  \end{center}  }
```

Note the sequence of commands in the first brace and second brace.

8.5 Going Further

As we near the end of this book, we now look at something which is a bit different than what is covered. TEX programming! The motive behind to introduce it at this point is, just to lead you through the path ahead. It is fine to skip this section if you are naive in LATEXbut remember to return and read it, once you get accustomed to using LATEX. We shall go through some commands by addressing a particular problem.

8.5.1 Problem

Consider a scenario where one attends a meeting, jots down some points, action to be taken by whom and by when, etc, which is then to be circulated to all concerned people. Usually, everyone gets a standard notepad or some kind of a book or diary for the meeting. To note down all points in an organized manner such that, it does not take time to compile it at the end of the day, one needs a personalized notepad to do so.

8.5.2 Approach

We would like to have a notepad with the following:

1. A title page

2. A page for important contact and team members

3. Multiple pages, say 100, each containing the following

   (a) Date, Start and end time, venue
   (b) List of attendees and absentees
   (c) Issue discussed, assigned to, and deadline
   (d) A random quote for motivation

Since concepts of point 1 and 2 are already covered in the earlier chapters, we shall skip them and shall proceed to address point number 3. Consider that a similar page given below is to be generated but 100 times.

Details

Date	Start:	End:
Venue:		
Attendees:		
Absent:		

Action Points

No.	Issue	Assignee	Deadline

" Think more, Speak less!"

Let's break down the problem into small components. (A) a page wrapper that will contain the subsequent components, (B) 'Details' part (C) the title 'Action Points' and the table header, (D) dotted lines, (E) quote.

A. Page Wrapper

```
\usepackage{tikz}
\foreach \pages
  in {1,...,100}
    {
  solve problem
  (B), (C), (D),
    (E)
}
```

foreach command is to execute everything given in the loop (mentioned in the curly brace) from 1 to 100. pages is a variable that will contain values from 1 to 100 as the loop iterates.

B. Details Part

This part is nothing much but a table containing the deails of the meeting like start and end time, venue, attendees, and absentees.

```
\section*{Details}
\renewcommand{\arraystretch}{1.5}
\begin{tabular}{p{4cm}p{3.5cm}p{3.5cm}}
  \hline
  \textbf{Date} & \textbf{Start:} &
    \textbf{End:} \\
  \hdashline[1pt/5pt]
  \textbf{Venue:} & & \\
  \hdashline[1pt/5pt]
  \textbf{Attendees:} & & \\
  \hdashline[1pt/5pt]
  \textbf{Absent:} & & \\
  \hline
\end{tabular}
```

C. Title and Table Header

This part, also like the previous one is a simple LaTeX table containing the table heading.

```
\section*{Action Points}
\begin{tabular}{lp{7cm}ll}
        \hline
        \textbf{No.} & \textbf{Issue} & \
           textbf{Assignee} & \textbf{
           Deadline} \\
        \hline
\end{tabular}
```

D. Dots to create line

In this part, we need dotted lines. hdashrule command is used for this purpose. The syntax is as follows

```
\usepackage{dashrule}
\hdashrule[VerticalSpace]{size}{thickness
   }{sizeOfEachDash SpaceBetweenEachDash}
```

15 such dotted lines are needed in our case. This will depend on the size of the page, margins, font size, etc. In this example, it is an A5 paper having 10 font size.

```
\foreach \rows in {1,...,15} {
   \noindent
   \hdashrule[5ex]{\textwidth}{0.5pt}{0.3
      mm 1mm}
}
```

E. Quote

(i) Defining and Reading array: Since we are generating 100 pages, assume that we have 100 quotes. We shall use an array to store these quotes and display them. The package, arrayjob is used. At first, a new array is defined using newarray command. Thereafter, readarray is used to store all the quotes.

```
\usepackage{arrayjob}
\newarray\Quote
```

```
\readarray{Quote}{
        Think more, Speak less!&
        Hard work always pays&
    ...
        Dream big
}
```

(ii) **Styling Quote:** Using the `newcommand` we will define the style of the quote. It has one argument which is the actual quote that will be displayed.

```
\newcommand{\randomquote}[1]
{\textit{\textsf{''#1''}} }
```

(iii) **Displaying Quote:** Finally we display the quote. `randomquote` is the new command defined with one argument. The argument is the array `Quote`. Each element of the array `Quote` is accessed with `pages` variable which goes from 1 to 100.

```
\randomquote{\Quote(\pages)}
```

Bibliography

[1] Font size. https://en.wikibooks.org/wiki/LaTeX/Fonts#Sizing_text, Feb 2016. [Online; accessed 17-Feb-2016].

[2] Comparison of tex editors. https://en.wikipedia.org/wiki/Comparison_of_TeX_editors, April 2018. [Online; accessed 6-April-2018].

[3] Document structure. https://en.wikibooks.org/wiki/LaTeX/Document_Structure, Feb 2016. [Online; accessed 10-Feb-2016].

[4] Page layout. https://en.wikibooks.org/wiki/LaTeX/Page_Layout, Feb 2016. [Online; accessed 15-Feb-2016].

[5] Footnotes and margin notes. https://en.wikibooks.org/wiki/LaTeX/Footnotes_and_Margin_Notes, Feb 2016. [Online; accessed 17-Feb-2016].

[6] Widows and orphans. https://en.wikipedia.org/wiki/Widows_and_orphans, Feb 2016. [Online; accessed 17-Feb-2016].

[7] Fonts. https://en.wikibooks.org/wiki/LaTeX/Fonts, Feb 2016. [Online; accessed 17-Feb-2016].

[8] Using colors. `https://en.wikibooks.org/wiki/LaTeX/Colors`, Feb 2016. [Online; accessed 17-Feb-2016].

[9] Formatting text. `https://en.wikibooks.org/wiki/LaTeX/Text_Formatting`, Feb 2016. [Online; accessed 17-Feb-2016].

[10] Walter Schmidt. Post script fonts and dingbats. `http://mirrors.concertpass.com/tex-archive/macros/latex/required/psnfss/psnfss2e.pdf`, September 2004. [Online; accessed 5-April-2018].

[11] Source code listings. `https://en.wikibooks.org/wiki/LaTeX/Source_Code_Listings`, Feb 2016. [Online; accessed 22-Feb-2016].

[12] Mathematics. `https://en.wikibooks.org/wiki/LaTeX/Mathematics`, Feb 2016. [Online; accessed 17-Feb-2016].

[13] Hiroshi Nakashima. Dashed lines. `http://texdoc.net/texmf-dist/doc/latex/arydshln/arydshln-man.pdf`, April 2016. [Online; accessed 28-Dec-2017].

[14] Images. `https://en.wikibooks.org/wiki/LaTeX/Importing_Graphics`, Feb 2016. [Online; accessed 27-Feb-2016].

[15] Andreas Matthias. Incldue pdf files. `http://texdoc.net/texmf-dist/doc/latex/pdfpages/pdfpages.pdf`, April 2016. [Online; accessed 28-May-2016].

[16] Hyperlinks. `https://en.wikibooks.org/wiki/LaTeX/Hyperlinks`, Feb 2016. [Online; accessed 28-Feb-2016].

[17] Sub version. `https://subversion.apache.org/`, April 2018. [Online; accessed 6-April-2018].

[18] Git hub. `https://try.github.io`, April 2018. [Online; accessed 6-April-2018].

[19] Git lab. `https://about.gitlab.com/`, April 2018. [Online; accessed 6-April-2018].

[20] Darcs. `http://darcs.net/`, April 2018. [Online; accessed 6-April-2018].

[21] Sharelatex. `https://www.sharelatex.com/`, April 2018. [Online; accessed 6-April-2018].

[22] Overleaf. `https://www.overleaf.com/`, April 2018. [Online; accessed 6-April-2018].

[23] Verbosus. `https://www.verbosus.com/`, April 2018. [Online; accessed 6-April-2018].

[24] Papeeria. `https://papeeria.com/landing`, April 2018. [Online; accessed 6-April-2018].

[25] F. J. Tilmann. Latex diff. `http://ctan.mirrors.hoobly.com/support/latexdiff/doc/latexdiff-man.pdf`, June 2017. [Online; accessed 6-April-2018].

[26] Macros. `https://en.wikibooks.org/wiki/LaTeX/Macros`, November 2017. [Online; accessed 10-May-2018].

Index

Printed in Great Britain
by Amazon